Washington Fish Species

Game Fish & Panfish

Billy Grinslott & Kinsey Marie Books

ISBN - 9781965098912

The Green Sunfish is blue green in color. It has yellow flecks on both its scales and some parts of its sides. The Green Sunfish also has broken blue stripes which is why some people confuse it with the Bluegill. Green Sunfish are very adaptable, they can live in any body of water that has vegetation or weeds.

Sculpins are small, bottom-dwelling fish with a flattened body shape, large pectoral fins, and a unique camouflage pattern, often found in clear, fast-flowing waters with rocky substrates, and they are known for their ambush hunting tactics. Sculpins have very large mouths and can swallow items nearly as large as themselves.

The burbot, also known as the eel pout. They get their name because they have a serpent-like or eel-like body. They can wrap their tail around things. There's nothing to worry about if you catch one, they may try to wrap their tail around your arm, but they are harmless. Burbots are adapted to cold water and are found in large, cold rivers, lakes, and reservoirs, primarily preferring freshwater habitats. Burbots are also known as eelpout, lingcod, and lawyer. The largest burbot caught in Washington state weighed 17.37 pounds.

The Rock Bass is not actually a bass but a member of the sunfish family. The biggest Rock Bass ever caught on record weighs about three pounds and was a little over one foot long. Rock bass prefer waters with rocky vegetated areas, that's how they got their name.

The bluegill also considered a sunfish is the most popular fish to fish for. They are called pan fish because they are about the size of a frying pan. Bluegills love to eat insects and bugs. They have good vision and rely on their keen eyesight to feed. Three types in this group are the Bluegill, Sunfish, and Pumpkinseed.

The Pumpkinseed is also known as pond perch, sun perch, and punky's sunfish. It can be found in numerous lakes, ponds, and rivers. It is their body shape resembling the seed of a pumpkin, that inspired their name. Pumpkinseed sunfish have speckles on their orangish colored sides and back, with a yellow to orange belly and chest. Pumpkinseeds can be found particularly in warmwater fisheries and other areas with similar habitats.

There are two main types of crapples. The white crappie and the black crappie. They are also members of the sunfish family. The difference between the white and black crappie is one has dark spots and the other has dark lines and is lighter in color. The white crappie has six dorsal fin spines, whereas the black crappie has eight dorsal fin spines. The white crappie can grow bigger and more of the bigger white crappie are caught in North America.

The Warmouth is a member of the Rock Bass, Green Sunfish and Bluegill family. They can survive in low oxygen environments while other fish cannot. Warmouth can thrive in muddy water, when other fish can't. Warmouth are often confused with rock bass. The difference between the two is in the anal fin: warmouth have three spines on the anal fin ray and rock bass have six spines.

Shad have exceptional hearing, including the ability to detect ultrasonic signals, which helps them navigate and avoid predators. Shad are energetic fighters and jumpers and have earned the nickname, the poor man's tarpon. Shad are anadromous, meaning they live in the ocean but migrate to freshwater rivers to spawn. The largest American shad ever recorded was two feet, six inches long.

The two most famous perches are the common perch and the yellow perch. The yellow perch has a brilliant greenish yellow color with orange fins. The yellow perch is the biggest one and can grow to a size of 18 inches. It's also known as the jumbo perch. The other type of perch is the white perch. The Washington State record for a yellow perch is 2.75 pounds.

Northern pikeminnows are voracious predators, consuming millions of young salmon and steelhead annually in the river systems. They occupy a wide variety of habitats, including deep river channels, river shorelines, and slow-water sloughs. They are fast swimmers, capable of reaching speeds of 10 miles per hour. They can grow up to 35 inches in length and 15 pounds in weight and can live at least 11 years. The largest Northern pikeminnow caught in Washington State weighed 7.92 pounds.

Whitefish are related to salmon and trout. They are known for their deep-bodied, silvery appearance and are a major part of the lake's ecosystem. They typically grow to 17-22 inches and range from 1.5-4 pounds. Whitefish are a popular and valuable commercial fish, generating income for commercial fisheries. Whitefish are also known as, whiting, and shad.

The largemouth bass is the most sought-after bass in North America. Largemouth bass live in just about every lake in North America. They have great hearing and can hear a crayfish crawling on the bottom of the lake. The state record largemouth bass weighed 12.53 pounds. It measured 23 inches long.

Smallmouth bass have a smaller mouth than the largemouth bass. They also have different markings and are lighter in color. They prefer living in colder water. They are typically found in the northern states in America because the water is cooler. The current world record smallmouth is an 11-pound, 15-ounce fish caught in Dale Hollow Lake. They can be found in lakes, reservoirs, and rivers. The largest smallmouth bass caught in Washington State was a 9-pound, 4-ounces, length 22 inches.

The black bullhead and yellow bullhead are part of the catfish family. They usually only grow to about 10 inches long. They use their whiskers to help find food. The bullhead is the most common member of the catfish family. Bullheads live in the water containing low oxygen levels. They can survive on low oxygen areas, where other fish can't.

There are several species of catfish. The Channel Catfish are the most fished catfish species with around 8 million anglers fishing for them per year. Channel Catfish have very few teeth and swallow their food whole. Channel catfish live in freshwater rivers, lakes, streams, and ponds. Catfish can live in low oxygen water, like bullheads. The largest channel catfish caught in Washington State is a 37.7-pound fish.

Sturgeons have sharp spines on their back, so be careful when handling them. Instead of scales, sturgeon skin is covered in bony plates called scutes, which can be very sharp on young sturgeon. Sturgeons have been around since the dinosaur days. Sturgeons mostly live in large, freshwater lakes and rivers. Their average lifespan is 50 to 60 years. The largest Sturgeon caught in Washington state weighed 670 pounds and measured 11 feet long.

The walleye got its name because of its white looking eyes. Their eyes collect light, even in low light conditions. This means they can see in the dark. Because they can see in the dark, they mostly feed at night. During the daytime their eyes are very sensitive, so they usually head for deeper water or shady places. Walleye like to live in cooler water and are normally found in the upper part of North America. They are found in various lakes and reservoirs. The largest walleye caught in Washington State weighed 20.32 pounds.

The Northern Pike is one of the most sought-after fish for anglers. It got its name because it likes to live in cooler water mainly in the northern states of North America. The northern pike is a very aggressive predator. They don't like to live in groups with other fish, they are very territorial and like to live alone. Their behavior is closely affected by weather conditions. Northern pike have eyes that can move in almost any direction. Northern pike can remain still for long periods of time. The largest Northern Pike caught in Washington State was a 34-pound, 6-ounce fish.

Another breed of the Muskie is the tiger muskie. The tiger muskie is a cross between the northern pike and muskie. They grow larger and faster than normal muskies and northern pikes. The tiger muskie got its name because it has tiger like stripes. Tiger Muskies are very rare and hard to catch. The largest tiger muskie caught in Washington State weighed 37.88 pounds and measured 50.38 inches in length.

Coastal cutthroat trout are native to the coastal streams and major rivers along the Pacific coast. These trout are also known as blueback trout or harvest trout. Some live mainly in freshwater areas, while others migrate to the ocean, particularly for feeding and refuge. They prefer cool, clean water with ample cover in rivers, lagoons, and small, low-gradient coastal streams. The Washington State Record Coastal Cutthroat Trout was a 12-pound fish.

Westslope cutthroat trout are common in river headwaters, lakes, and streams. They thrive in streams with more pool habitat and cover, than streams with very few pools and little or no cover. The average size of westslope cutthroat trout ranges between 6 to 16 inches in length. They can swim faster than rainbow trout, with a maximum speed of 11 feet per second. The largest Westslope cutthroat trout caught in Washington State weighed 4.71 pounds.

Mature Golden trout have a deep olive-green back that fades to bright gold on the sides, a vibrant red-orange lateral line, and black speckles near the tail. Golden trout are native to the remote waters at elevations of 6,000 to 10,000 feet. Golden trout, typically average 6 to 12 inches in length. The largest Golden trout caught in Washington State weighed 3 pounds, 12.96 ounces.

The cutthroat's name comes from the bright red or orange slash-like markings under their jaws. There are several subspecies of cutthroat trout, including the coastal, Yellowstone, and Lahontan cutthroat. They inhabit a variety of cold, freshwater environments, including small streams, rivers, and lakes. Mature cutthroat trout can range from 6 to 40 inches in length. The largest cutthroat trout caught in Washington State was a Lahontan Cutthroat Trout, weighing 18.04 pounds.

Bull trout thrive in cold, clean, and complex aquatic habitats, with water temperatures ideally below 55°F. Some bull trout are anadromous, meaning they migrate from freshwater to saltwater for part of their life cycle, and then return to freshwater to spawn. Bull trout usually grow to a common length of around 25 inches, with the maximum reported length being 40.5 inches. They are found in high-alpine lakes and streams. The largest bull trout caught in Washington State was 23 pounds, 2 ounces.

Yellowstone cutthroat trout are distinguished by prominent red slashes on their lower jaws, large black spots, and orange to drab coloration. They inhabit relatively clear, cold streams, rivers, and lakes. They typically measure from 6 to 30 inches long when they reach maturity. The largest Yellowstone cutthroat trout caught in Washington State weighed 27 pounds 6 ounces.

Steelhead are rainbow trout that migrate to the ocean and then return to their freshwater spawning grounds. Steelhead and rainbow trout are genetically identical, the difference lies in their lifestyle, with steelhead migrating to the ocean and rainbow trout remaining in freshwater. The Washington State record for a steelhead was a 35-pound, 1-ounce fish.

Brown trout can live up to 20 years. Brown trout have higher tolerance for warmer waters than either brook or rainbow trout. Brown trout can be found on almost every continent except Antarctica, and many can be found living in the ocean. The largest Brown Trout caught in Washington State was a 22-pound fish.

The rainbow trout gets its name because of its brilliant colors. Rainbow trout populations are good indicators of water pollution because they can only survive in clean waters. They like to live in rivers and streams. Rainbow trout rank among the top five most sought game fish in North America. The state record for rainbow trout in Washington State is a 25.45-pound fish.

Brook trout are characterized by their olive-green bodies with pale, worm-like markings, red spots with bluish halos, and orange-red fins with white and black edges. They can grow up to 12 inches in length. Brook trout are cold-water fish that prefer clean, clear, and cold streams, lakes, and ponds. The largest Brook trout caught in Washington State was a 9.00-pound fish.

The primary salmon species you'll find are landlocked sockeye salmon, also known as kokanee. These are the non-anadromous form of sockeye salmon, meaning they don't migrate to the ocean. They live their entire lives in freshwater lakes and reservoirs. The largest sockeye salmon caught in Washington State had a length of 31 inches and a weight of 14 pounds 13 ounces.

Pink salmon have the shortest lifespan of any Pacific salmon species, living only two years. The pink color of their skin comes from the crustaceans they eat, which are rich in a reddish-orange pigment. Pink salmon are one of the most abundant species of Pacific salmon. Pink salmon hatch in freshwater streams and migrate to the ocean after a few months. The largest pink salmon caught in Washington State was a 15.4-pound fish, 31 inches long.

Chum salmon, also known as dog salmon, are a common Pacific salmon species. They are the most widely distributed of all Pacific salmon species, found in coastal streams from Arctic Alaska to San Diego, California. Chum salmon have a dark olive-green back and dark maroon sides, with irregular greenish vertical bars on the sides, and no spots on the back or tail. Chum salmon are medium-sized fish, averaging 24 inches in length and between 9.7 to 22 lbs. in weight. The largest chum salmon caught in Washington state weighed 25.97 pounds.

The Arctic grayling is one of the most beautiful freshwater fishes. Its most striking physical feature is the large, sail like dorsal or backfin. The Arctic grayling comes in a wide array of colors. Their color can vary from stream to stream. The sides of the body, fins and head can be freckled with spots. They can grow to be 30 inches long and weigh up to 8.4 pounds. They can travel more than 100 miles in one year. The largest recorded Arctic grayling is 8.4 pounds and 30 inches in length.

The lake trout is one of the biggest of the trout family. The biggest lake trout caught was 72 pounds. Lake trout like to live in lakes that are deep. They like being in the cool water in the deep parts of a lake. They have been reported to live up to 70 years in some Canadian lakes. The largest lake trout caught in Washington State weighed 31 pounds, 2.75 ounces.

Coho salmon, also known as silver salmon, are fish that live in both freshwater and saltwater, migrating from the ocean to their natal streams to spawn, where they die shortly after. Some coho salmon migrate more than 1,000 miles in the ocean, while others remain in marine areas close to the streams where they were born. Adult coho salmon typically weigh 8 to 12 pounds and are 24 to 30 inches long, but some can reach up to 36 pounds. The largest Coho salmon caught in Washington State weighed 25.27 pounds.

Chinook also known as the king salmon are the most widespread Salmon in North America. Chinook salmon are hatch in freshwater streams and rivers then migrate out to the saltwater environment of the ocean to feed and grow. Chinook salmon are the largest of the Pacific Ocean salmon, that's how they got the name king salmon. The largest chinook salmon caught in Washington weighed 68 lbs. 4.16 oz.

Fun Facts About Washington Fish

1 - The steelhead is the State Fish of Washington. The State record for a steelhead is a 35-pound, 1-ounce fish.

2 - The largest fish caught in Washington State was a white sturgeon weighing 670 pounds and measuring 11 feet long.

3 – While migrating to their spawning areas, salmon can leap waterfalls up to eight feet high.

4 - There are five species of Pacific salmon found in Washington, chinook, coho, chum, sockeye and pink.

5 - In Washington State, the most popular fish for anglers are rainbow trout and Steelhead.

6 - Washington State has 7 thousand lakes and 4 thousand rivers statewide for fishing.

7 – Washington state has 67 different species of fish. With 37 being native and 30 introduced or stocked.

Author Page

Billy Grinslott & Kinsey Marie Books

ISBN – 9781965098912

Thanks

www.ingramcontent.com/pod-product-compliance
Lightning Source LLC
Chambersburg PA
CBHW060852270326
41934CB00002B/107

* 9 7 8 1 9 6 5 0 9 8 9 1 2 *